Arranged by MELODY BOBER

The Songs of Johnny Mercer

John Herndon "Johnny" Mercer is one of the most prolific lyricists in history, having written the words for more than 1,000 songs. He collaborated with many of Hollywood's greatest composers including Harold Arlen, Hoagy Carmichael, Dorothy Fields, Jerome Kern, Henry Mancini, and Jimmy Van Heusen, to name a few. Additionally, timeless legends like Louis Armstrong and Frank Sinatra to contemporary artists like Michael Bublé and Eva Cassidy have performed and recorded his songs, four of which won Academy Awards: "On the Atchison, Topeka and the Santa Fe" (1946) from *The Harvey Girls;* "In the Cool, Cool, Cool of the Evening" (1951) from *Here Comes the Groom;* "Moon River" (1961) from *Breakfast at Tiffany's;* and "Days of Wine and Roses" (1962) from *Days of Wine and Roses.*

These beautiful arrangements by Melody Bober are perfect piano solos for lessons, recitals, or social gatherings. To show the clever brilliance of Mercer's craft, the lyrics have been included. The gentle melody of "Skylark," the humor in "You Must Have Been a Beautiful Baby," and all of the other wonderful musical moments are certain to provide hours of enjoyment for the pianist who wishes to be a *Popular Performer.*

CONTENTS

Blues in the Night

Lyrics by Johnny Mercer
Music by Harold Arlen
Arr. Melody Bober

blow - in' 'cross the tres - tle, whoo - ee._____ (My

ma - ma done tol' me.)_____ A whoo - ee - duh - whoo - ee._____ Ol'

click - et - y clack's a - ech - o - in' back th' blues._____

ped. ad lib.

8va

COME RAIN OR COME SHINE

Lyrics by Johnny Mercer
Music by Harold Arlen
Arr. Melody Bober

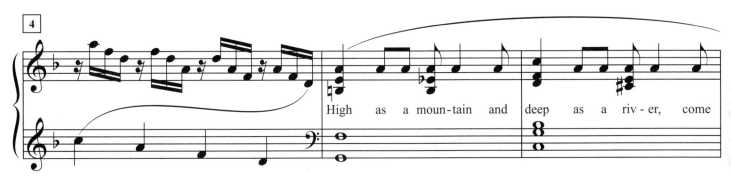

I'm with you al-ways, I'm with you rain___ or shine!

With energy (♩ = 92)

DAYS OF WINE AND ROSES

Lyrics by Johnny Mercer
Music by Henry Mancini
Arr. Melody Bober

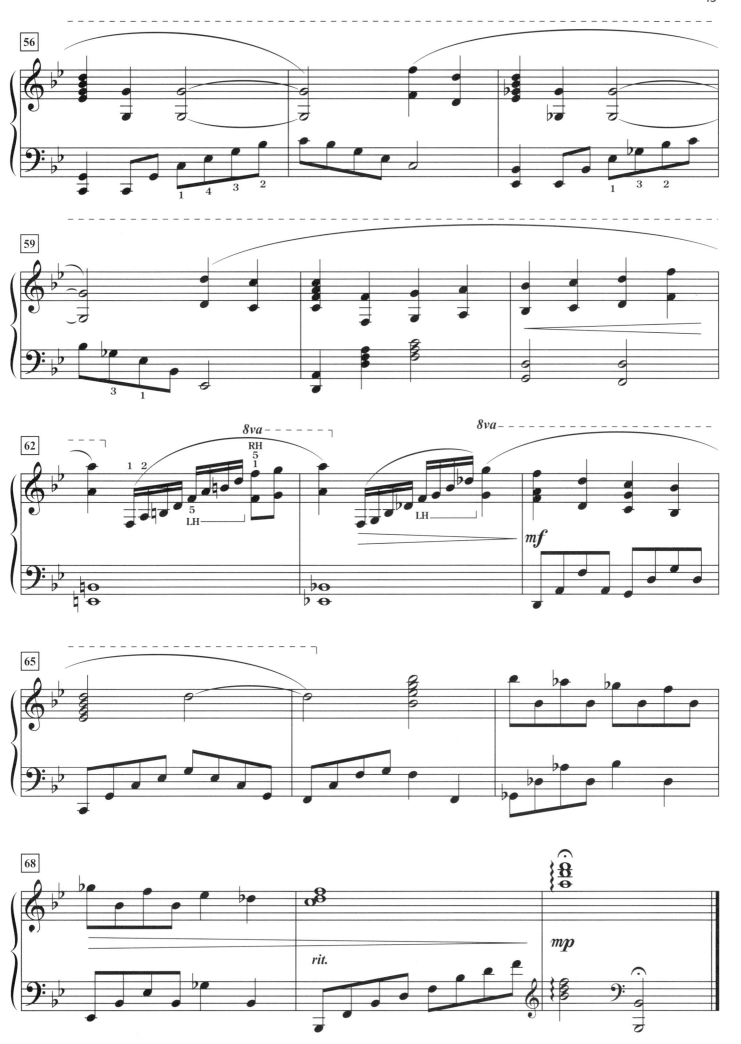

THE GLOW WORM

Music by Paul Lincke
Modern Version by Johnny Mercer
Original Words by Lilla Cayley Robinson
Arr. Melody Bober

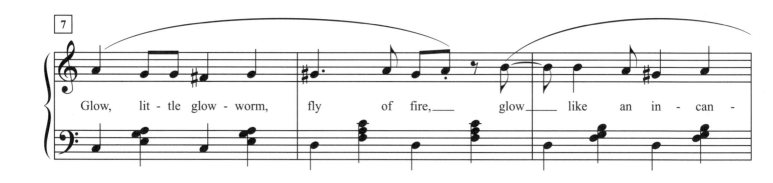

Glow, lit - tle glow - worm, fly of fire,___ glow___ like an in - can -

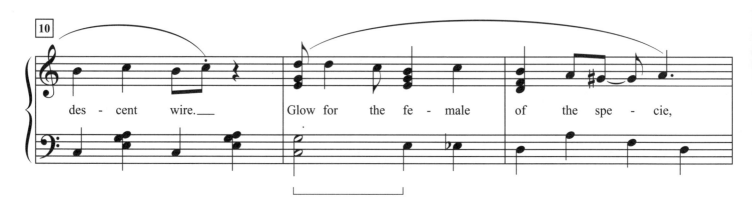

des - cent wire.___ Glow for the fe - male of the spe - cie,

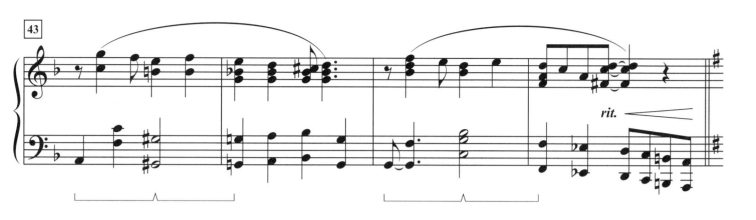

Broadly (♩ = 104)

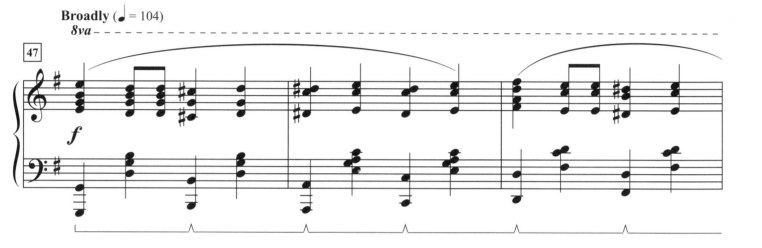

Tempo I

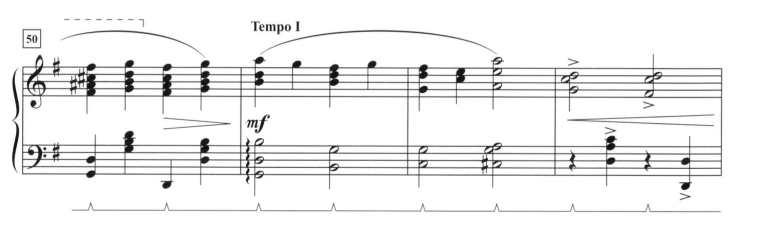

Hooray for Hollywood

Lyrics by Johnny Mercer
Music by Richard A. Whiting
Arr. Melody Bober

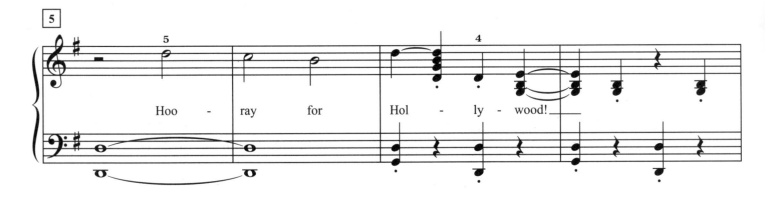

Hoo - ray for Hol - ly - wood!

That screw - y bal - ly - hoo - ey Hol - ly - wood,

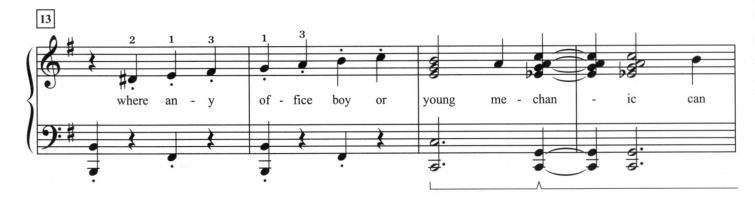

where an - y of - fice boy or young me - chan - ic can

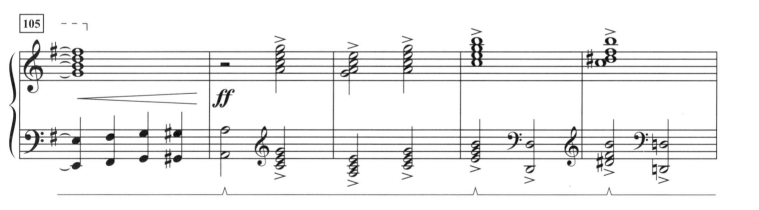

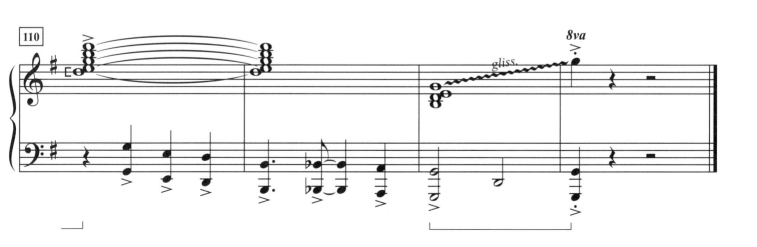

Jeepers Creepers

Lyrics by Johnny Mercer
Music by Harry Warren
Arr. Melody Bober

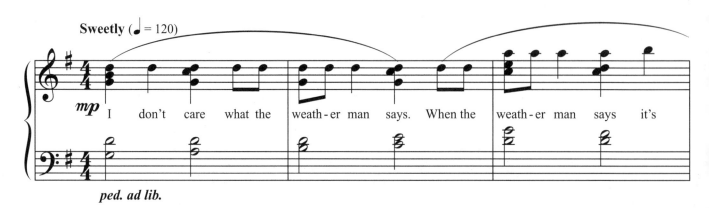

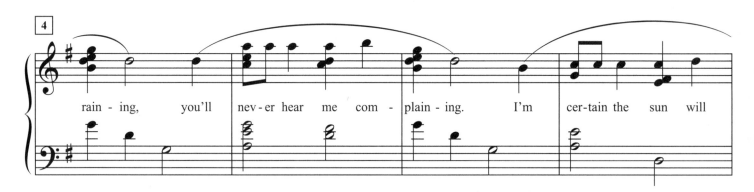

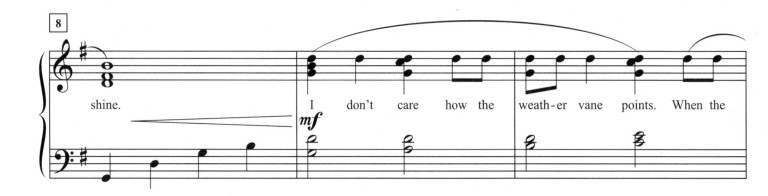

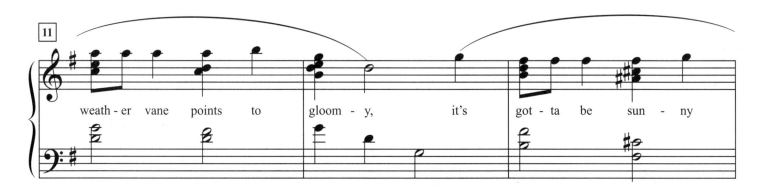

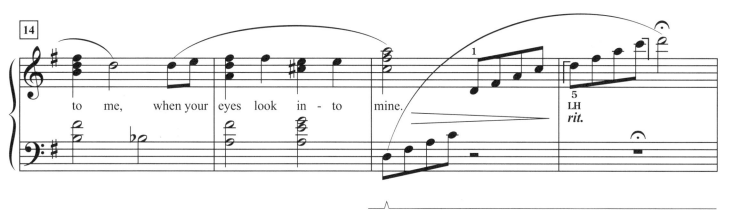

to me,   when your eyes look in - to   mine.

With energy (♩ = 144)

Jeep - ers___   Creep - ers!___   Where'd ya get those   peep - ers?___

Jeep - ers___   Creep - ers!___   Where'd ya get those   eyes?

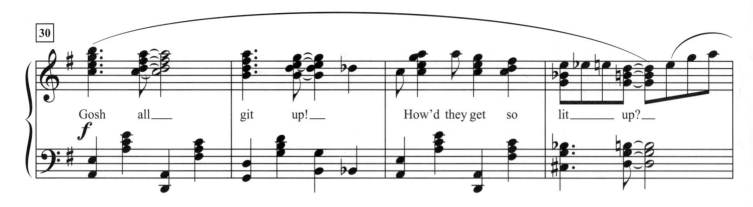

Gosh all___ git up!___ How'd they get so lit___ up?___

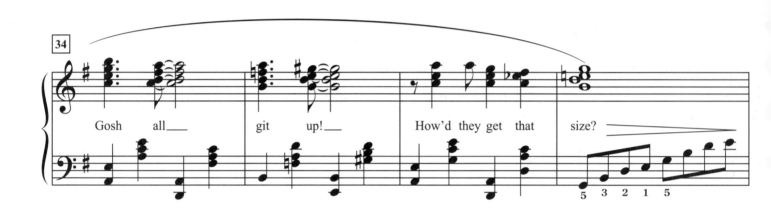

Gosh all___ git up!___ How'd they get that size?

lightly

Gol - ly gee! When you turn those heat-ers on,___

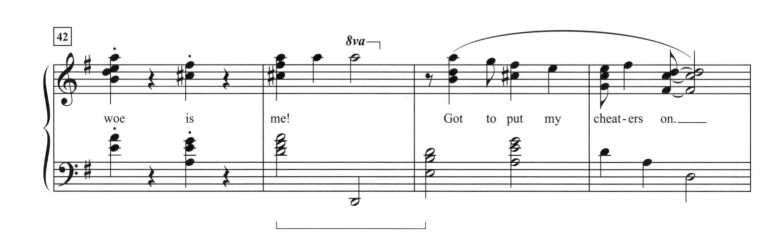

woe is me! Got to put my cheat-ers on.___

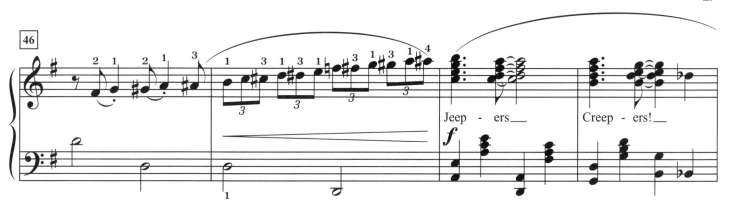

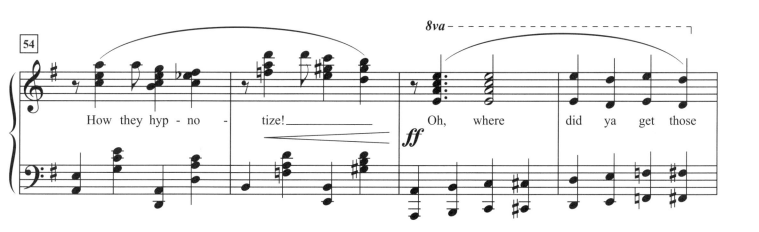

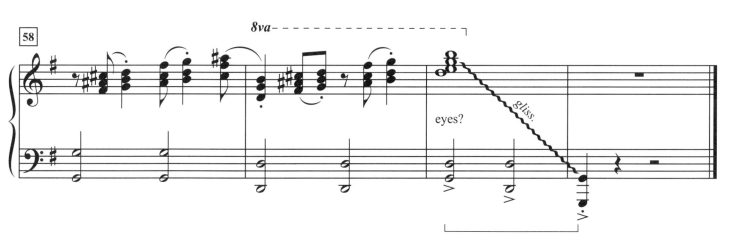

On the Atchison, Topeka and the Santa Fe

Lyrics by Johnny Mercer
Music by Harry Warren
Arr. Melody Bober

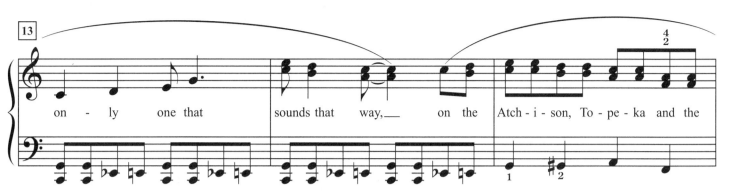

on - ly one that sounds that way,___ on the Atch - i - son, To - pe - ka and the

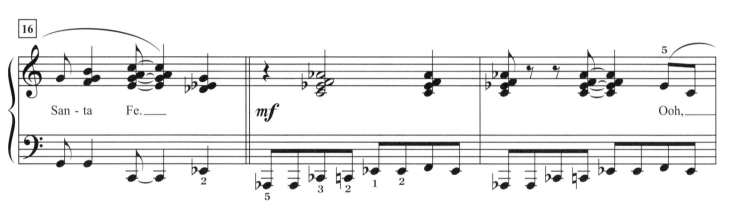

San - ta Fe.___ *mf* Ooh,___

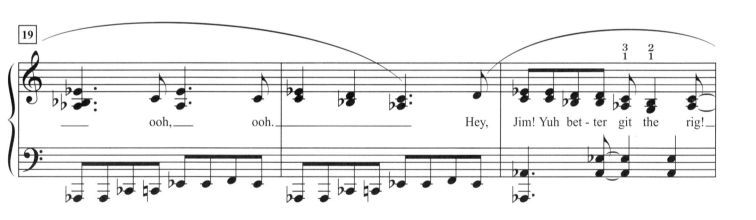

___ ooh,___ ooh.___ Hey, Jim! Yuh bet - ter git the rig!___

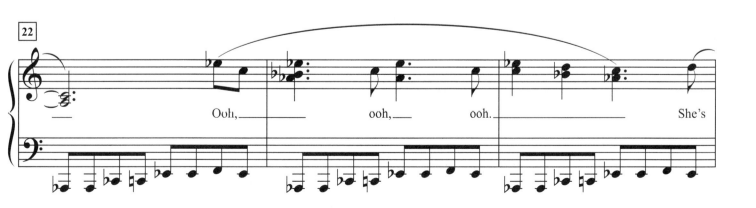

___ Ooh,___ ooh,___ ooh.___ She's

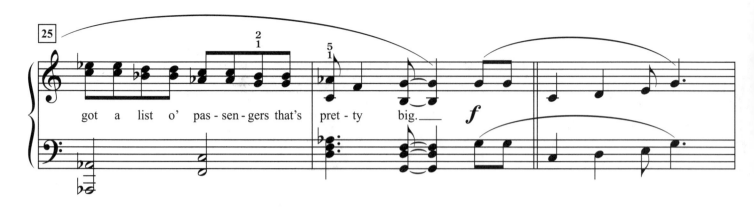

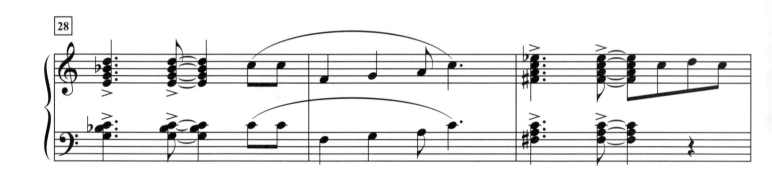

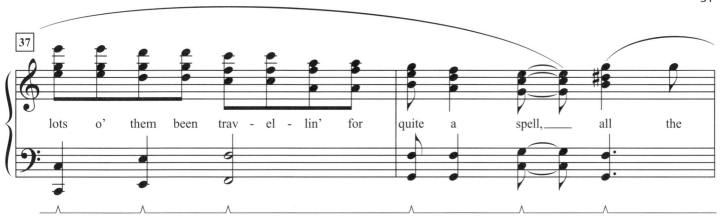

lots o' them been trav - el - lin' for quite a spell,____ all the

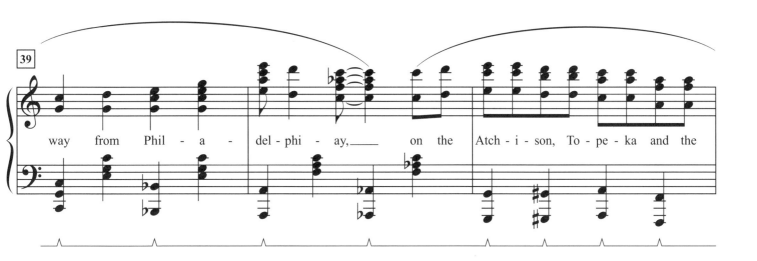

way from Phil - a - del - phi - ay,____ on the Atch - i - son, To - pe - ka and the

Tempo I (♫ = ♫)

San - ta Fe.

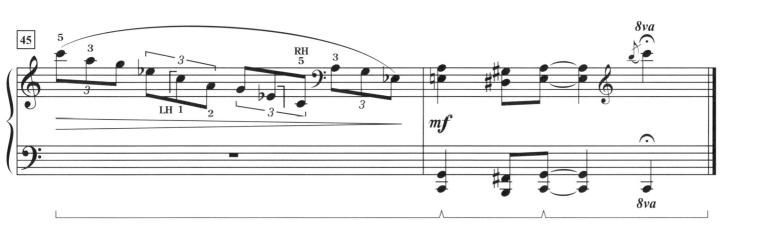

mf

SKYLARK

Lyrics by Johnny Mercer
Music by Hoagy Carmichael
Arr. Melody Bober

Sky - lark, have you seen a val - ley green with spring,

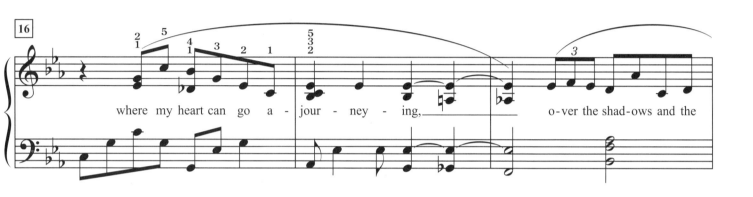

where my heart can go a - jour - ney - ing,_____ o-ver the shad-ows and the

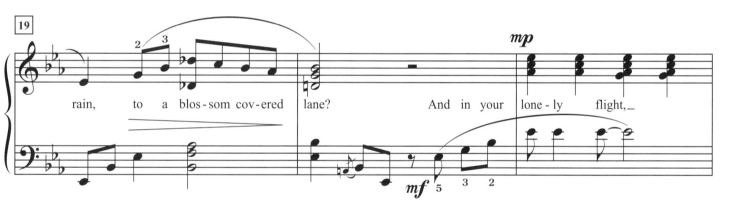

rain, to a blos-som cov-ered lane? And in your lone - ly flight,_

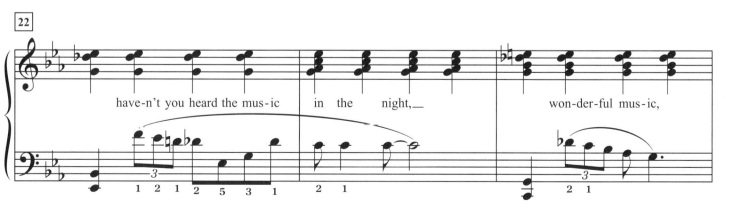

have-n't you heard the mus-ic in the night,_ won-der-ful mus-ic,

34

…won't you lead me there?

SUMMER WIND

Music by Henry Mayer
English Lyrics by Johnny Mercer
Original German Lyrics by Hans Bradtke
Arr. Melody Bober

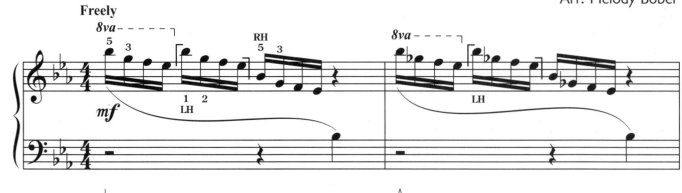

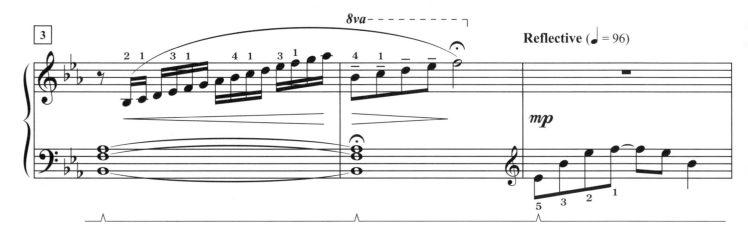

You Must Have Been a Beautiful Baby

Lyrics by Johnny Mercer
Music by Harry Warren
Arr. Melody Bober

must have been a beau - ti - ful ba - by 'cause baby look at you

rit.

Medium swing (♩ = 100)

now!

mf

f